Mother

Original title, *Cuore di Mamma*
© Edizioni San Paolo, Italy, 1999
Edited by Tiziano Daniotti
Illustrations by Anna Luisa Durante,
Rosella Monfrino and See Sun Roo

Translated into English and edited by
Michael Goonan,
© St Pauls Publications, 2007

AUSTRALIAN edition published by
ST PAULS PUBLICATIONS
PO Box 906
Strathfield NSW 2135 Australia
ISBN 978 1 921032 28 8

UK-Ireland edition published by
ST PAULS Publishing
187 Battersea Bridge Rd,
London SW11 3AS, UK
ISBN 978-85-439-7260-?

ST PAULS is an activity of the priests and brothers
of the Society of St Paul who proclaim the Gospel
through the media of social comunication.

A Mother's Heart

ST PAULS

Mother,
when we were little children
we thought
you knew everything.

With the passing of years
we have come
to appreciate you
for who you are:
a human being
like all of us
who has good days
and bad days,
and sometimes gets it wrong.

What sets you apart
is your never-failing love for us.

We know you loved us
from the first moment
you held us in your arms,
and that you have loved us
ever since.

The sacrifices you
lovingly made
while we were growing up
can never be repaid.

All the mothers of the world
are beautiful,
but you, Mother,
are the most beautiful of all.

In your heart

The cornerstone of the house,
the most important part,
is not found in the earth,
but in the mother's heart.

Lydia O. Jackson

*M*other's love is peace.
It need not be acquired,
it need not be deserved.

Eric Fromm

There are many beautiful things
that God can give us twice.
But a mother is something so great
that she can be given
to us only once.

Harriet Beecher Stowe

*W*here did it bloom,
that shining freshness
on the cheeks of a child?
From the mother
who was carrying the child
in her heart,
silent gift of her purity,
delicate mystery of her love.

Rabindranath Tagore

The most beautiful masterpiece
of the heart of God
is the heart of a mother.

Therese of Lisieux

*To be a mother
is an absolute mystery,
a mystery beyond compare,
an absolute relative to nothing.
A work impossible yet complete.*

Christian Bobin

The ear of the mother
is so close to her heart
that she is able to hear
even the softest whisper
of her baby.

Kate Douglas Wiggin

ALWAYS WITH YOU

A mother helps you
when others ignore you,
encourages you
when others mock you,
defends you
when others condemn you,
accepts you
when others reject you.

Daniel P. Cronin

*A baby is someone
who lives within you
for nine months,
in your arms for three years
and in your heart
until death.*

M. Mason

*What the mother sings
the cradle
goes all the way down
to the coffin.*

Henry Ward Beecher

The word 'mother'
is hidden in the heart
and comes to the lips
in moments of grief
and happiness,
as perfume rises from the heart
and blends with fresh air.

Kahlil Gibran

The most important thing
a father can do
for his children
is to love their mother.

Theodore Hesburgh

*It is an immense miracle
for a mother
to see and hold in her arms
a being who was formed
within her.*

Simone de Beauvoir

Youth fades; love droops;
the leaves of friendship fall.
A mother's secret hope
outlives them all.

Oliver Wendell Holmes Jr

$\mathcal{I}$n this cold and empty
world,
the only fountain
of strong love,
deep and without end,
is found in the heart
of a mother.

Felicia Hemans

THANK YOU, MOTHER

I love my mother
as the trees love water
and sunshine -
she helps me grow, prosper,
and reach great heights.

Adabella Radici

I am so tired that I feel feint.
Then I stop for a moment
and I look at the photo
of my three little ones
playing by the seashore.
And I smile.
And I thank God
for my children.

Janina McLeod

I love people. I love my family,
my children...
but inside myself is a place
where I live all alone
and that's where I renew
the springs that never dry up.

Pearl S. Buck

$\mathcal{A}$ mother's arms
are made of tenderness
and children
sleep soundly in them.

Victor Hugo

*W*hen God thought of mother,
he must have laughed
with satisfaction,
and framed it quickly.
So rich, so deep, so divine,
so full of such beauty,
was the conception.

Henry Ward Beecher

A man loves
his sweetheart the most,
his wife the best,
but his mother the longest.

Irish Proverb

$\mathcal{L}$ove is the only thing
that increases
when we share it
without reservation.

Ricarda Huch

WITH A SMILE

*G*od could not be everywhere,
so he created mothers.

Jewish Proverb

A mother is a woman
with twenty-five hours
of work to do in a day,
yet she will always find
a free hour to play
with her children.

Iris Peck

In its better moments,
motherhood is spontaneous
like a beautiful
burst of laughter.
It is an automatic,
unintentioned
and unconditional love.

Sally James

*Every beetle is a gazelle
in the eyes
of its mother.*

Moorish Proverb

The hand that rocks
the cradle
is the hand that rules
the world.

William Ross Wallace

She is beautiful
for the care
she shows to her baby.
Mothers have this beauty
which comes from love,
as the day comes from the sun,
as the sun comes from God.

Christian Bobin

$\mathcal{W}$hat you keep for yourself
you have lost already.
What you give away
will be yours forever.

Josef Recla

SWEET MEMORIES

$\mathcal{Y}$ou were getting up
at dawn
to leaven the bread
with the love
of your hands.

Giovanni Campus

*W*ho ran to help me
when I fell,
and would some
pretty story tell,
or kiss the place
to make it well?
My mother.

Ann Jane Taylor

*M*y mother had a great deal
of trouble with me,
But I think she enjoyed it.

Mark Twain

*M*y mother used to say,
'He who angers you,
conquers you'.
But my mother was a saint.

Elizabeth Kenny

I remember, Mother,
your two hands on my head,
ruffling my hair,
the unexpected tenderness
of those hours
filled with light.

Ottaviano Menato

A mother's happiness
is like a beacon,
lighting up the future,
but reflected also
on the past
in the guize
of fond memories.

Honoré de Balzac

*M*other,
you never seemed
to be surprised
by what was happening.
True?
Even this was beautiful to us.

Alberto Bevilacqua

LIKE YOU

O Mother,
I know all the times
that you generated me.
In silence.
Not seen by anyone.
You wanted me beautiful,
equal to the son of Mary.

Davide Turoldo

Woman, you are so great
and valuable,
that anyone who seeks grace
and does not come to you
wants to fly without wings.

Dante Alighieri

*N*ear to the cross of Jesus
stood his mother,
and the sister of his mother.
Jesus, seeing his mother
and the disciple
he loved, said:
'Woman, behold your son'.

The Gospel of John

*M*other of Christ,
I do not come to pray.
I have nothing to offer you
and nothing to ask.
O Mother, I come
only to be able to look at you.

Paul Claudel

*M*other of heaven,
nearer to God than we are,
extend your blessed hands,
your marvelous
and loving hands,
full of light, over us.

S. Lawrence

CONTENTS